Bogdan Patrut
Tiberiu Socaciu

Dynamic Data Structures

Bogdan Patrut
Tiberiu Socaciu

Dynamic Data Structures

Lists, Stacks, Queues, and Trees

Lehrbuchverlag

Impressum/Imprint (nur für Deutschland/only for Germany)
Bibliografische Information der Deutschen Nationalbibliothek: Die Deutsche Nationalbibliothek verzeichnet diese Publikation in der Deutschen Nationalbibliografie; detaillierte bibliografische Daten sind im Internet über http://dnb.d-nb.de abrufbar.

Coverbild: www.ingimage.com

Verlag: Der Lehrbuchverlag ist ein Imprint der
Südwestdeutscher Verlag für Hochschulschriften GmbH & Co. KG
Heinrich-Böcking-Str. 6-8, 66121 Saarbrücken, Deutschland
Telefon +49 681 37 20 271-1, Telefax +49 681 37 20 271-0
Email: info@verlag-lehrbuch.de

Herstellung in Deutschland:
Schaltungsdienst Lange o.H.G., Berlin
Books on Demand GmbH, Norderstedt
Reha GmbH, Saarbrücken
Amazon Distribution GmbH, Leipzig
ISBN: 978-3-8417-6004-3

Imprint (only for USA, GB)
Bibliographic information published by the Deutsche Nationalbibliothek: The Deutsche Nationalbibliothek lists this publication in the Deutsche Nationalbibliografie; detailed bibliographic data are available in the Internet at http://dnb.d-nb.de.

Cover image: www.ingimage.com

Publisher: Lehrbuchverlag
is an imprint of the publishing house
Südwestdeutscher Verlag für Hochschulschriften GmbH & Co. KG
Heinrich-Böcking-Str. 6-8, 66121 Saarbrücken, Deutschland
Phone +49 681 37 20 271-1, Fax +49 681 37 20 271-0
Email: info@verlag-lehrbuch.de

Printed in the U.S.A.
Printed in the U.K. by (see last page)
ISBN: 978-3-8417-6004-3

Scientific referee: Dr. Iulian-Marius Furdu

Translated from Romanian language by Ruxandra Alexandru

Table of Contents

Foreword

The purpose of this book is: a) to make students understand the difference between static and dynamic variables and the role of the pointer variables; b) to point out the advantages of the dynamic allocation; c) to present the different types of data structure dynamically linked; d) to identify the optimally solvable problems using different types of dynamic structures.

All problems are solved in Turbo Pascal language, because it is familiar to many students. The programming language that is used here is less important because this is a book about data structure and programming technique.

While reading, it can be found several images that might help the reader (teacher or student) for his study work.

Thus, the following symbols mean class type or teaching method, especially for the class itself, and are recommended for teachers:

Speaking Methods

Discussion Methods

Students´ Independent Reading

Laboratory Class

Students´ Examination and Grading Class

Remarks and Comments about the Specific Purposes of a Chapter or Class

There are also other symbols that mark students´ activities.

☞ Remark whose aim is to clarify difficult or peculiar aspects from the text

🔔 Pay Attention! Pay attention to some important aspects; don´t rush otherwise you might solve the problem superficially

? Questions and self-check exercises, of four different levels:

☺ (basic level) 😐 (intermediate level)

☹ (advance level) 💣 (proficient level)

We want to say that these symbols, together with the images and explanations from every problem, will turn this book into a useful course book, not only for students but also for those specialists who are interested in the programming techniques, for those who don´t limit themselves just to the knowledge of a certain programming language.

The given symbols are neither mandatory requests from teachers nor from the students, they are just recommendations for readers.

It is suggested trying other methods that can be interesting for students.

Having said all these, we hope this work will be useful for all readers.

Dr. Iulian-Marius Furdu

"Vasile Alecsandri" University of Bacau, Romania

Chapter 1. Reference Type. The Concept of Dynamic Variable

As you know, a graph can be memorized as an adjacency matrix. But, if the graph has a lot of nodes, the use of the adjancency matrix is useless.

Also, if we want to create a program for a highschool competition, the data storage for the applicants is not possible with vectors, because we cannot declare vectors of similar lengths to real situations (500 competitors, for instance). So, we should have a new data structure, a sort of *list,* that could store more information which is linked between them, in a larger memory space.

There are also some situations when we need special data structure, for instance, to memorize a seldom hierarchy, like a genealogical tree. For such cases and not only, the data structures, called *statics*, are not very helpful. All these disadvantages can disappear once we use the *dynamic* data structures.

1.1. Static Variables and Dynamic Variables

The variables can be *static* or *dynamic*. Those which are static are allocated during compilation, in well-defined memory spaces. The structure, type and their place from the memory cannot be modified while the program is running. All the variables that we have used in simple programs with vectors were static.

The Pascal Language gives the chance of allocating the memory while the program is running, for some variables called dynamic variables, depending on the case, and it also frees the memory which was occupied by them. The type of the **dynamic** variables must be well defined, but these ones will not be declared in "var" section. Also, the access to these variables is not made directly. They are given a **reference** type in the correspondence, in a biunivoc way, which is said to refer or point to that dynamic variable.

The reference type variable can have references only to the dynamic variable which was allocated to it correspondingly. The reference is done by storing the address, where the dynamic variable is stocked, in the reference variable. The correspondence between the dynamic variable and the reference type allows the understanding of the dynamic variable structure.

During compilation, a 4-bytes space, which has the memory address of the dynamic referred variable, will be allocated for the reference variables.

The dynamic variables are allocated in a memory space called **heap**, different from the fixed zone of the program, where the static variables are memorized.

A referred dynamic variable will occupy a memory space according to its type: 2 bytes for `Integer`, 6 bytes for `Real`, 10 bytes for a `string` of 9 characters (`String[9]`) etc.

1.2. Defining a Reference Type

You can define a sort of reference in `type` section like:

```
type referential_type = ^dynamic_variable_type
```

(symbol "^" is read "pointer at...").

The set of type_reference values is made of an unlimited number of addresses. Every address identifies a type_variable_dynamic variable. Then it is added a special value, called **`Nil`**, which does not identify any variable to this union of values.

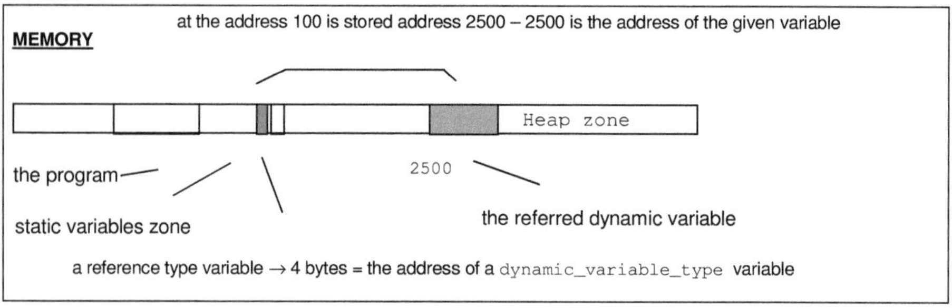

Example:

```
type pReal = ^Real;
var pr: pReal;
```

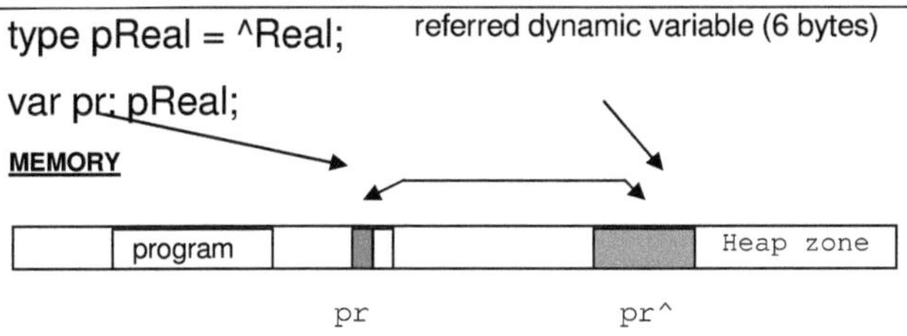

It is possible that, when coming across the type of the dynamic variable, its type should not be known yet (reference beforehand); this type must be declared later, in the same declaration of type.

Example:

```
type p_complex = ^complex;
        complex = record re, im: Real end;
var r1, r2: p_complex; r3: ^complex; r4: ^Char;
```

The possibility of using types that refer to themselves (are defined recursively) – the so-called linked types – is another facility of this language:

```
type list = ^article;
     article = record
                  a, b: Integer;
                 next: list
              end;
var l: list;
```

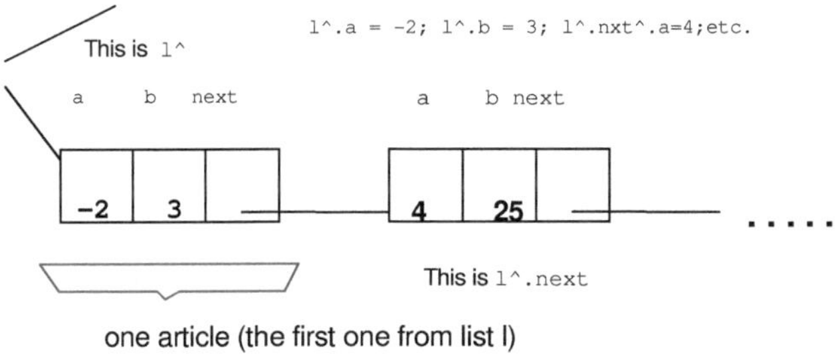

1.3. The Use of Dynamic Variables. Advantages

A dynamic variable can be memorized in two steps:

- the allocation of the memory space for a dynamic variable, using the **New** procedure;

- the actual storage, meaning to store the data of that certain dynamic variable to the address.

The **Dispose** procedure is used to free up the memory space of one dynamic variable, which is occupied with New procedure.

Example:

```
program TestPointer;
type complex = record
                re, im: Real
              end;
     pComplex = ^complex;
var pz: pComplex;
begin
   New(pz); pz^.re:=1.2; pz^.im:=5.6;
   WriteLn('Complex number: ',pz^.re, ' ', pz^.im);
   Dispose(pz); ReadLn
end.
```

All the operations that can be executed with data of that certain type can be performed employing the dynamic variables.

There are several advantages when using the pointers. For instance:

- the use of a reduced memory space, if complex data structures are used.
- the more efficient use of the memory space, if reusing it (after Dispose), since it is possible to do so.

Example

```
type person = record
                   familyname, firstname: String;
```

```
                    {2*256 bytes = 512 bytes}
                  age: Integer
                    {2 bytes, total of 514 bytes}
                end;
      pPerson = ^person; { 4 bytes }
      set_pers_1 = array[1..50] of person;
      set_pers_2 = array[1..50] of pPerson;
var M1: set_pers_1; {50*514=25700 bytes}
    M2: set_pers_2  {50*4=200 bytes, the rest is in the
heap !}
```

? Questions and answers

1 ☺ How many types of variables do you know in the Pascal language?

2 😐 What is a dynamic variable?

3 ☹ Where are the dynamic variables stored? Are they declared in the "`var`" section?

4 ☹ What is a reference type? How is this connected to a basic type?

5 ☹ How is allocated the memory of a dynamic variable? What is the purpose of the `Dispose` procedure?

6 ☹ What are the advantages when using dynamic allocated data?

7 💣 Write a program that can operate on a crowd of people, making use of the notions in the final paragraph: reading, addition, elimination, search of people.

Chapter 2. Lists

2.1. Basic operations: insertion, search and elimination of an element

Let´s consider the last example from the previous section. In order to overcome the disadvantage of the big size of vectors (50 elements), we make a linked list, in which every single article (node) of the list contains information about one person.

```
type pPerson = ^person;
     person = record
                    familyname, firstname: String[20];
                    age: Integer;
                    next: pPerson
          end;
var first, last: pPerson;
{the element from beginning and the element from the end}
```

Using these declarations, we make a list of persons and then we search for a certain person in the list.

```
program WithDynamicList;
type pPerson = ^person;
     person = record
                familyname, firstname: String[20];
                age: Integer; next: pPerson
               end;
var n,p: String[20]; v: Integer;
    found: Boolean; answer: Char;
     first, current: pPerson;
begin
  first:=Nil;
```

```
  repeat
    Write('Family name='); ReadLn(n);
    Write('First name='); ReadLn(p);
    Write('Age='); ReadLn(v);
    New(current);
    with current^ do
         begin
           familyname:=n;
           firstname:=p;
           age:=v;
           next:=first
         end;
    first:=current;
    Write('Do you continue [Y/N]? '); ReadLn(answer)
  until answer in ['n','N'];
  Write('First searched family name = '); ReadLn(n);
  current:=first; found:=False;
  while (current<>Nil) and (not found) do
    if current^.familyname=n then
       gasitfounde
       current:=current^.next;
  if found then
    WriteLn('First name=',current^.firstname,
            ', age=',current^.age)
  else
    WriteLn('Person not found in the list...');
  ReadLn
end.
```

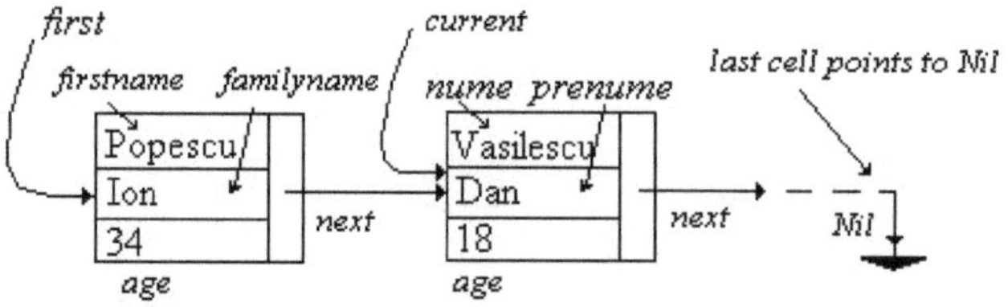

In this program, we created the section that can add an element in front of the list which was already created.

```
So, we have:
```

It is allocated memory for a new element:

```
New (current);
```

It is written the data for a new element:

```
with current^ do
     begin
         familyname:=n;
         firstname:=p;
         age:=v;
```

... and it is added in front of the list which was already created.

```
         next:=first
       end;
```

Then, the new beginning of the list will be exactly this element:

```
first:=current;
```

Then, let´s rewrite the program so that we can remove a certain element, given from the keyboard. In order to remove the first element, we add in front of the list, after this one was created, an unnecessary element, because the list will be covered differently, using one element “behind”.

So, the element to remove will be `current^.next`, in order to link the `current^` with `current^.next^.next^`.

```
program RemoveFromList;
type pPerson = ^person;
     person = record
```

```
                familyname, firstname: String[20];
                age: Integer; next: pPerson
               end;
var n,p: String[20]; v: Integer;
    found: Boolean; answer: Char;
    first, current, to_remove: pPerson;
begin
  first:=Nil;
  repeat
    Write('Family name='); ReadLn(n);
    Write('First name='); ReadLn(p);
    Write('Age='); ReadLn(v);
    New(current);
    with current^ do
         begin
           familyname:=n; firstname:=p;
           age:=v; next:=first
         end;
    first:=current;
    Write('Do you continue [Y/N] ? '); ReadLn(answer)
  until answer in ['n','N'];
  Write('Family name to remove? = '); ReadLn(n);
  New(current); current^.next:=first;
  found:=False;
  while (current^.next<>Nil) and (not found) do
    if current^.next^.name=n then
       found:=True
    else
       current:=current^.next;
  if found then
```

```
      begin
        to_remove:=current^.next;
        Write('Removing ');
        Write(to_remove^.familyname,' ',
              to_remove^.firstname);
        WriteLn(' with age ',
                to_remove^.age,' years.');
        current:=current^.next^.next;
        Dispose(to_remove)
      end
   else
     WriteLn('Person not found in the list...');
   ReadLn
end.
```

? Questions and exercises

1 ☺ Write a program that can read the data of some persons from a text file (the given data are: first name, second name and age) and that can list the last and first names of all the persons that are over 18.

2 ☹ Make a list of real numbers, which are read from the keyboard, until number 0 is found. Also, decide how many of them are integers.

3 ☹ Whole numbers are read from the keyboard until 0 is found. Make a list of these numbers. Decide how many of these consecutive pairs of numbers from the list are prime.

4 💣 Make a list of characters, `L`, which are read from the keyboard, then make an M list that has the characters from `L, set in reverse order.`

2.2. Stacks and Queues. Specific operations

Dynamic lists are very useful when you deal with a lot of information, which the vectors are incapable of stocking, or inefficient in trying to do so.

The stacks and queues are particular cases of simple-linked lists. These ones use different in and out mechanisms. For each of them, a node of the list represents a record that contains an information (`info`), and also a pointer (indicator) for the previous or for the next element in list (`prev` or `next`).

General Overview

- A **stack** is a dynamic data structure represented by an simply-linked list, where the in and out mechanism of the elements is LIFO – meaning that the last one to enter is the first one which gets out (last in – first out). So, we record a stack like this:

```
type Stack = ^Cell;
     Cell = record
              info: Integer; { information }
              prev: Stack
            { previous element from the stack }
            end;
var S: Stack;
```

So, you need only a single pointer for the first element of the heap in order to add an element (this step being called Push) or to eliminate (Pop) it, because both of these operations are carried out in the superior part of the list.

•**Queue** is a dynamic data structure represented by a simply-linked list where the in and out mechanism is FIFO - meaning that the last one which gets in is the first one which gets out (last in – first out). So, we save a queue like this:

```
type  PCell = ^Cell;
      Cell = record
               info: Integer; { information }
               next: PCell { next element from queue }
             end;
      Queue = record first, last: PCell end;
var Q: Queue;
```

So, for a queue, we need two pointers, one for the first element of the queue (*the head of the queue*) and another one for its last element (*the end of the queue*), since the insertion in the list is made at the back of it, and the elimination in front of it.

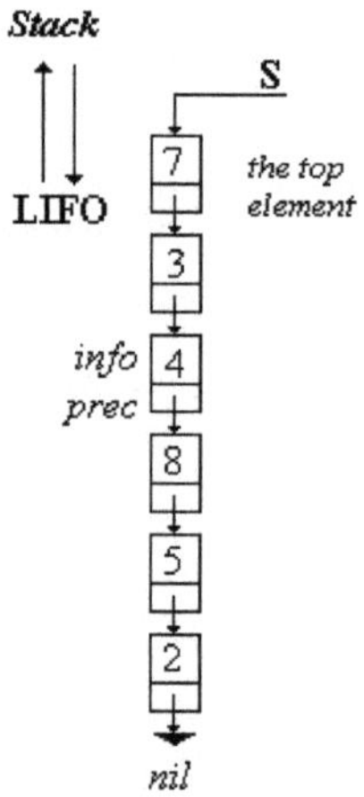

the stack will be displayed as: > 7, 3, 4, 8, 5, 2

Queue

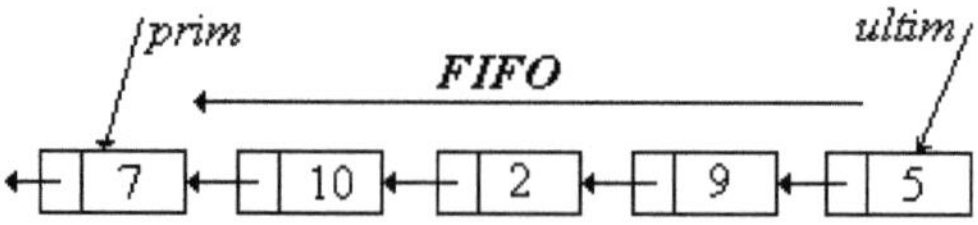

7, 10, 2, 9, 5

Demonstrative Programs

We present two experimental programs that use these data structures. The elements from the list are whole numbers. The insertion of an element is made simply by writing the number, but the element must be neither 0 nor -1. The elimination of the element (according to the LIFO and FIFO mechanism) is made introducing -1. The program is stopped if 0 is introduced.

1. The Program with Stacks. By using Init(s), you start making a stack `S`. By using `Push(S,elem)` you can add the integer element `elem` to the stack `S` and when using `Pop(S,elem)` you can eliminate the element `elem` from the stack `S`.

```
program WithStack;
type Stack = ^Cell;
     Cell = record
                 info: Integer;
                 prev: Stack
               end;
procedure Init(var S: Stack);
begin S := Nil end;
procedure Push(var S: Stack; elem: Integer); { put }
var C: Stack;
begin
  New(C);
  C^.info := elem;
  C^.prev := S; S := C
end;
procedure Pop(var S: Stack; var elem: Integer); {extract}
var C: Stack;
begin
  if S = Nil then
```

```
      begin
        Write('Empty stack ...');
        elem := -1
      end
   else
      begin
        C:=S; elem:=C^.info; S:=C^.prev; Dispose(C)
      end
end;
procedure Display(S: Stack);
var C: Stack;
begin
  C := S;
  Write('The stack is: ',#16);
  while C <> Nil do
        begin
          Write(C^.info,',');
          C := C^.prev
        end;
  WriteLn
end;
var S: Stack; elem: Integer;
begin
  Init(S); Display(S);
  repeat
    Write('Give the element (-1 = pop, 0 = stop): ');
    ReadLn(elem);
    if elem <> 0 then
     if elem <> -1 then
        begin
```

```
          Push(S,elem);
          Display(S)
        end
     else
      begin
        Pop(S,elem);
        WriteLn('Poped: ', elem);
        Display(S)
      end
  until elem = 0;
end.
```

2. The Queue Program. This one works as the previous one, except that the insertion and elimination procedures are called `Put` and `Get`, and the mechanism that facilitates these operations is called FIFO.

```
program QithQueue;
type PCell = ^Cell;
     Cell = record
                info: Integer;
                next: PCell
              end;
     Queue = record
               first,last:PCell
             end;
procedure Init(var Q: Queue);
begin
  New(Q.first); New(Q.last);
  Q.first^.next:=Q.last;
  Q.last^.next:=C.first
end;
```

```
procedure Put(var Q: Queue; elem: Integer);
var P: PCell;
begin
  New(P); P^.info:=elem;
  P^.next:=Nil;
  if Q.first=nil then
     {no element}
     begin
       Q.first:=P; Q.last:=P
     end
  else
     begin
       Q.last^.next:=P;Q.last:=P
     end
end;
procedure Get(var Q: Coada; var elem: Integer);
var P: PCell;
begin
 P := C.first;
 if C.first = Nil then
  begin
    Write('Empty queue ...'); elem := -1
  end
 else
  begin
    elem := Q.first^.info;
    Q.first := Q.first^.next;
    Dispose(P)
  end
end;
```

```
procedure Display(Q: Queue);
var P: PCell;
begin
  Write('The queue is: ');
  P := Q.first;
  while P <> Nil do
        begin
          Write(P^.info,',');
          P := P^.urm
        end;
  WriteLn
end;
var Q: Queue; elem: Integer;
begin
  Init(Q); Afis(Q);
  repeat
    Write('Give the element (-1 = get, 0 = stop): ');
    ReadLn(elem);
    if elem <> 0 then
      if elem <> -1 then
        begin
          Put(Q,elem); Display(Q)
        end
      else
        begin
          Get(Q,elem); WriteLn('We obtain: ', elem);
          Display(Q)
        end
  until elem = 0;
end.
```

2.3. Doubly-linked list. Specific Operations

Unlike the stacks and queues, the double-linked lists have new elements:

- there are two specials pointers beginning and ending, which point out through two extreme cells, but they are not a part of the list; these are called *sentinels*;
- there is a pointer called `current` that always shows the current element from the list;
- every element of the list is linked to the elements before and after it with two pointers: `prev` and `next`;
- there is a field `len` that shows the length of the list.

Thus, the list of numbers 1,2,3 will be memorized like in the following figure:

The operations required in the case of such a list are:

- initializing the list;
- adding an element at the end of the list;
- inserting an element before the present element from the list;
- erasing the present element from the list;
- displaying the list.

When you add or insert a new element in the list, that element becomes the current one. When the current element is erased from the list, its place is taken by the element that succeeds it in the list.

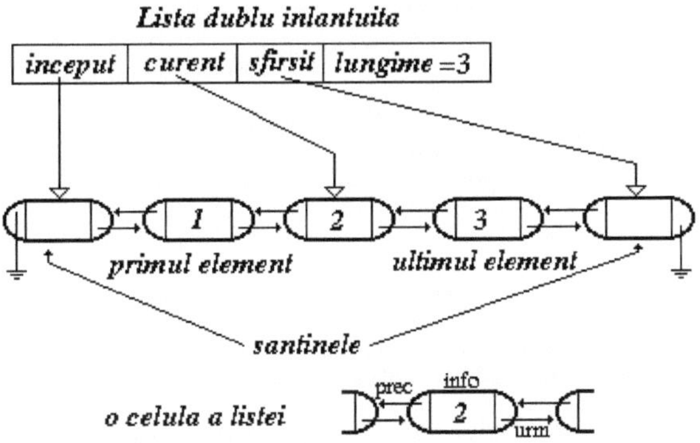

When you insert or remove an element from the list, some links disappear while others appear.

For instance, let´s say we have one L list and the information is inserted before the present element. Then we create a new cell, called C, to which we will add this information. We call the present cell A and the one after it B. Then, we have to break the links between A and B while creating links between A and C and between C and B. Also, the length of the list will increase by 1. These facts are highlighted in the following procedure and in the image as well.

```
procedure Insert(var L: List; elem: type_of_info);
var A,B,C: PCell;
begin
      New(C);
      A:=L.current;
      B:=L.current^.urm;
      C^.info:=elem;
      C^.prev:=A;
      C^.next:=B;
      A^.next:=C;
      B^.prev:=C;
      L.len:=L.len+1;
      L.current:=C
end;
```

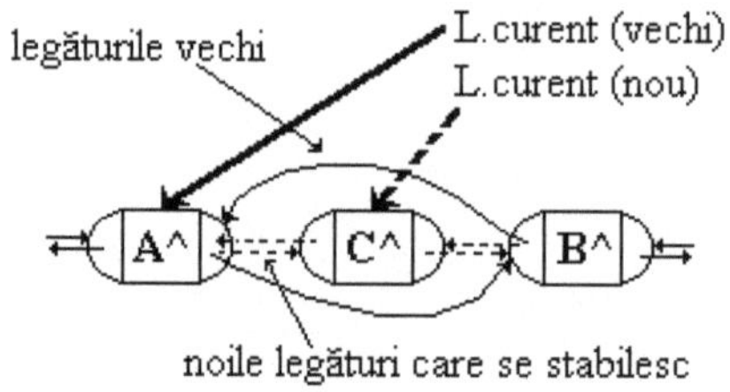

Almost reverse processes take place when eliminating the present element from the list. Obviously, this can be done only if the list is not void. To actually free the memory space up after eliminating the element that has occupied it, the Dispose procedure will be used. Removing the current element involves linking the element that precedes it with the one that succeeds it.

```
procedure Delete(var L: List);
var C: PCell;
begin
  with L do
    if len>0 then
      begin
        C:=current;
        C^.prev^.next:=C^.next;
        C^.next^.prev:=C^.prev;
        current:=C^.next; Dispose(C);
        len:=len-1
      end
end;
```

The successor of the removed element becomes the current element. Also, the length of the list decreases by one unit.

In the following part, we present a program for the admission to high school. The applicants are placed in a dynamic double-linked list. Thus, the number of applicants will be limited only by the available memory of the computer, so it can be very large, in comparison to the situation of storing the students in an array.

To sort the students fulfilling a certain criterion (alphabetically or considering the average grade, in descending order), we used a version of the sorting algorithm, ``*bubble sort*``, that uses a list L instead of a vector. Basically, the algorithm is the same. The differences come up when you cover the list and in the case of the elements to be compared: instead of `x[i]` and `x[i+1]`, you compare `L.current^.info` şi `L.current^.urm^.info`, which are in fact those key fields when sorting. In the program, the sequence that uses the bubble sort algorithm is bordered.

```
{$X+}
program WithLists;
uses Crt;
type student = record name: String;
                      score1, score2, average: Real end;
     tip_info=student;
     PCell = ^Cell;
     Cell = record
                info: tip_info;
                prev, next: PCell
              end;
     List = record
                first, current,  last: PCell;
                len: Integer
             end;
procedure Init(var L: List);
begin
  with L do
     begin
       len:=0;
      New(first); New(last);
```

```
        first^.next:=last;
        first^.prev:=nil; last^.prev:=first;
        last^.next:=Nil; current:=first
      end
end;
```
procedure GoFirst(var L: List);
```
begin
  while not (L.current=L.first^.next) do
        L.current:=L.current^.prev
end;
```
procedure Add(var L: List; elem: tip_info);
```
var C: PCell;
begin
  New(C);
  with C^ do
    begin
      info:=elem;
      prev:=L.last^.prev;
      next:=L.last^.prev^.next
      { sau L.last}
    end;
  with L do
    begin
      len:=len+1; last^.prev^.next:=C;
      last^.prev:=C; current:=C
    end
end;
```
procedure Remove(var L: List);
```
var C: PCell;
begin
```

```
  with L do
    if len>0 then
       begin
         C:=current;
         C^.prev^.next:=C^.next;
         C^.next^.prev:=C^.prev;
         current:=C^.unext; Dispose(C); len:=len-1
       end
end;
```
procedure Insert(var L: List; elem: tip_info);
```
var A,B,C: PCell;
begin
  New(C);
  A:=L.current;
  B:=L.current^.next;
  C^.info:=elem;
  C^.prev:=A;
  C^.next:=B;
  A^.next:=C;
  B^.prev:=C;
  L.len:=L.len+1;
  L.current:=C
end;
```
procedure Display(L: Lista);
```
var i: Integer;
begin
  GoFirst(L); i:=1;
  while not (L.current = L.last) do
    begin
      with L.current^.info do
```

```
        WriteLn(i,'. ',name:20,
                score1:6:2,score2:6:2, average:6:2);
      L.current:=L.current^.next; i:=i+1
    end;
  WriteLn('Total : ',i-1,' students.')
end;
procedure AddStudent(L: List);
var E: student;
begin
  WriteLn('Add student');
  with E do
    begin
      Write('Name : ');
      ReadLn(nume);
      Write('Scores : ');
      ReadLn(score1,score2);
      media:=(score1+score2)/2
    end;
  Add(L,E)
end;
procedure RemoveStudent(var L: List);
var the_name: String; found: Boolean;
begin
  WriteLn(Remove student'); PozitioneazaLaInceput(L);
  WriteLn('Name : ');
  ReadLn(the_name); found:=False;
  while (not (L.current = L.last)) and (not found) do
    if L.current^.info.name = the_name then
       found:=True
    else
```

```
      L.current:=L.current^.next;
  if found then
     Remove(L)
  else
     WriteLn('We didn't find this student...')
end;
```

procedure SearchStudent(L: List);

```
var the_name: String; found: Boolean;
begin
  WriteLn('Search student'); GoFirst(L);
  WriteLn('Name : '); ReadLn(numele);
  found:=False;
  while (not (L.current = L.last)) and (not found) do
    if L.current^.info.nume = the_name then
      found:=True
    else
      L.current:=L.current^.next;
  if found then
     with L.current^.info do
          WriteLn(name,' ',
                  score1:6:2,score2:6:2,average:6:2)
  else
     WriteLn('This student is not in the list...')
end;
```

procedure ListStudentsByNames(L: List);

```
var ready: Boolean; aux: student;
begin
  WriteLn('List students by name');
  { bubble-sorting the students}
  repeat
```

```
    ready:=True;
    GoFirst(L);
    while not (L.current^.next=L.last) do
      begin
        if L.current^.info.name >
           L.current^.next^.info.name then
           begin
             ready := False; aux := L.current^.info;
             L.current^.info:=L.current^.next^.info;
             L.current^.next^.info:=aux
           end;
        L.current:=L.current^.next
     end
  until ready;
  Display(L) { display the list }
end;
procedure ListStudensByAverages(L: List);
var ready: Boolean; aux: student;
begin
  WriteLn('List students by averages');
  {bubble-sort method}
  repeat
    done:=True; {starting with the first position
                 = at the begining, traverse the list}
    GoFirst(L);
    while not (L.current^.next=L.end)do
      begin
        if L.current^.info.average
             < L.current^.next^.info.average
           then
```

```
          begin
            done := False; aux := L.current^.info;
            L.current^.info:=L.current^.next^.info;
            L.current^.next^.info:=aux
          end;
        L.current:=L.current^.next
      end
  until done;
  Display(L)
end;
var L: Lista; option: Char;
begin
  Init(L);
  repeat
    ClrScr;WriteLn('Menu:');WriteLn;
    WriteLn('1 = add student');
    WriteLn('2 = delete student');
    WriteLn('3 = find student');
    WriteLn('4 = list by name');
    WriteLn('5 = list by averages');
    WriteLn('0 = stop program');
    WriteLn; Write('Option=');
    ReadLn(option); ClrScr;
    case option of
         '1': AddStudent(L); '2': RemoveStudent(L);
         '3': SearchStudent(L);
         '4': ListStudentsByNames(L);
         '5': ListStudentsByAverages (L)
    end;
    if option in ['1'..'5'] then ReadKey
```

```
 until option='0'
end.
```

2.4. Circular Lists

In a circular list, the last element is linked to the first one:

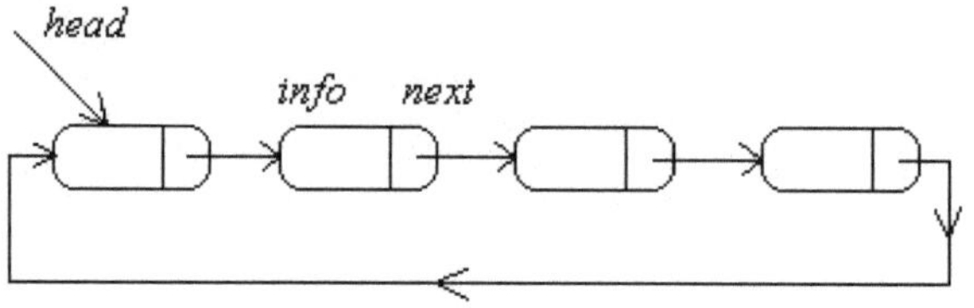

The next program makes a circular list and displays it:

```
program CircularList;
type list = ^cell;
     cell = record
                 info: Char;
                 next: list
               end;
var head, p, q: list; { head = list head }
    i,n: Integer; { n = nr. of current elements from the
list }
begin
     WriteLn('Circular list'); WriteLn('***************');
     Write('Give the nr. of elements: '); ReadLn(n);
     Write('Give the first info: ');
     New(head); ReadLn(head^.info);
     head^.next:=head;
     for i:=2 to n do
         begin
           Write('Give the ',i,'-th info: ');
           New(p);
           ReadLn(p^.info);
```

```
          q:=head^.next;
          p^.next:=q;
          cap^.next:=p;
          head:=p
        end;
    head:=head^.next;
    WriteLn('Display the list: ');
    p:=head;
    repeat
      Write(p^.info,'->');
      p:=p^.next
    until p=head;
    Write(p^.info);
    ReadLn
end.
```

In the following part we present a program with circular double-linked lists. There is one N number of kids sitting in a circle. At one moment, starting with the m kid, the k kid is removed from the circle, the circle becoming narrower. You are asked to display the order in which the kids are removed from the circle, considering n, m, k and the direction in which the circle is covered. For instance, for n=5, m=3, k=2 and the left-hand side, you will get the following order: 3, 5, 2, 1, 4.

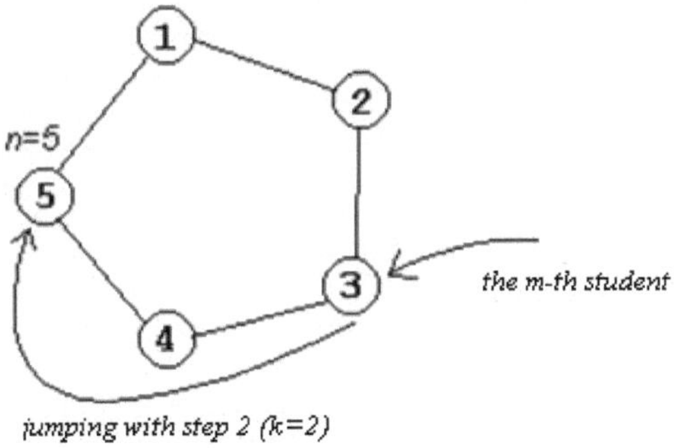

```
program DoubleLinkedCircularLists;
type list=^cell;
     cell=record
              info: Integer;
              prev,next: list
            end;
var head,p,q: list;
    dir: Char; i,j,n,m,k: Integer;
begin
     Write('Doubly-linked circular lists. ');
     WriteLn('Example');
     Write('Give the nr. of children: '); ReadLn(n);
     Write('Give the start child: '); ReadLn(m);
     Write('Give the ratio: '); ReadLn(k);
     { put element 1 in the list }
     New(p); p^.info:=1; p^.next:=p; p^.prev:=p;
     head:=p; {the list starts with head and ends with p}
     { put the other elements in list }
     for i:=2 to n do
         begin
           New(q);
           q^.info:=i; p^.next:=q;
           q^.prev:=p; q^.next:=head;
           p:=q
         end;
     while head^.info<>m do head:=head^.next;
     Write('Give the direction to move [l,r]: ');
     ReadLn(dir);
     for i:=1 to n do
         begin
```

```
        WriteLn('Remove the child nr. ', head^.info);
        p:=head; p^.prev^.next:=p^.next;
        p^.next^.prev:=p^.prev;
        case dir of
             'l': head:=head^.prev;
             'r': head:=head^.next
        end;
        Dispose(p);
        { jump over the other k children }
        for j:=1 to k do
            case dir of
                 'l': head:=head^.next;
                 'r': head:=head^.prev
            end
      end;
   ReadLn
end.
```

The composed statement that adds a new element to the list is:

```
begin
  New(q);
  q^.info:=i;
  p^.next:=q;
  q^.prev:=p;
  q^.next:=head;
  p:=q
end;
```

This one can be graphically represented as:

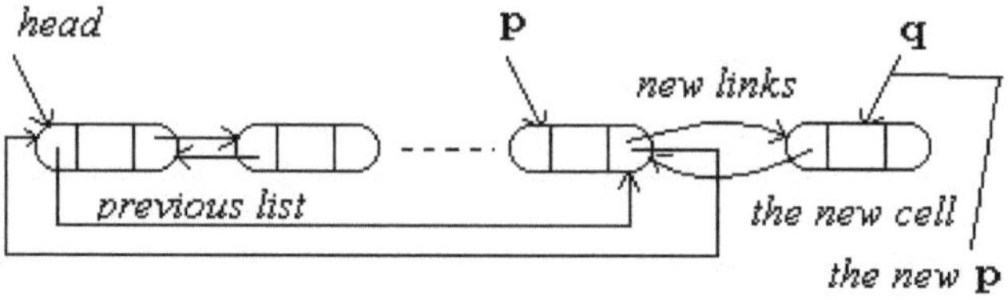

Create procedures for different operations that use circcular lists: creating, displaying, deleting an element, adding an element etc.

2.5. Topological Sort

Let´s consider T = a set of terms (words) from a certain field. We want to include them in a dictionary in which, when defining any of the terms, the terms from T, to which this definition can be applied, have appeared previously. In this way, we will obtain a report of partial order: we will say that a<b (a and b belonging to T) if the term a appears in the definition of b.

The problem that is raised is that the terms have to be sorted in the dictionary in such a way that if a comes up before b, then either a<b, or a and b are not comparable. This is a **topological sort** of the elements from T.

The problem does not always have a solution. So, if T={a,b,c} and a<b<c<a, we cannot sort T topologically.

We can represent the order reports between two elements a and b of T with an arrow (oriented arc) from one top that is labeled a to another one with b.

Thus, for example, for T={a,b,c,d,e,f,g,h} and e<b, c<b, c<d, b<d, b<a, a<f, d<f, f<h, a<h, a<g relations, we make a digraph (oriented graph) like:

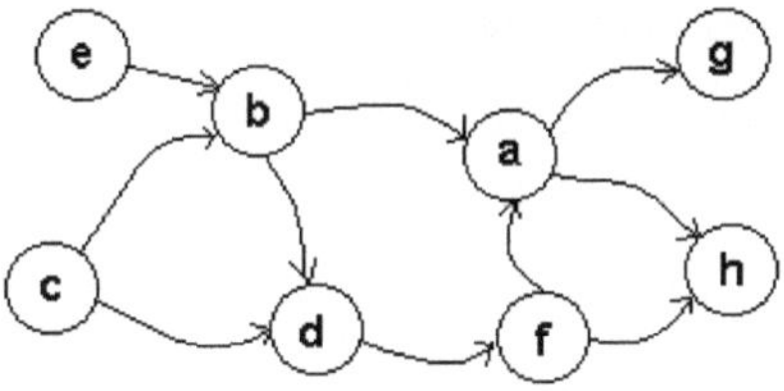

The concept of oriented graph (or digraph) will be studied in *The Foundations of Informatics.*

The topological sort of the *n* elements is done in n steps: at every `i` step, a *j* term is displayed and removed from the digraph whose property is that no arc should come into contact with its corresponding point.

In order to do this, we need to have for every j term a list of its successors, meaning those k elements having the property of that `term[j]<term[k]`.

Let´s consider `list_succ[j]` the list of the successors of term f.

To test if a node has or not arcs that enter it, we need to keep a number (`nr_pred[j]`) that shows the number of the predecessors of the terms from that node.

To eliminate a term j from the digraph you need to eliminate its vertex (node) and all the arcs that set out from that node. Also, these operations can be expressed like this:

• removing the vertex:

```
nr_pred[j]:=-1
```

• for any element from the list of the j successors, the number of its predecessors decreases by one unit.

```
p:=list_succ[j];
while p<>Nil do
  begin
    nr_pred[p^.info]:=nr_pred[p^.info]-1;
    p:=p^.next
  end
```

Adding a<b in digraph involves:

- b is added to the list of the succesors of a.

```
New(p); p^.info:=k2;p^.next:=list_succ[k1];
list_succ[k1]:=p;
```

- the number of the predecessors of b is increased.

```
nr_pred[k2]:=nr_pred[k2]+1
```

The following program solves the topological order problem. In the case of the example in the image, we get e, c, b, d, f, a, g, h.

```
program TopologicalSort;
const max=10;
type pTop=^Top; { reference to Top }
     Top=record { an element of the lists of successors }
                info: Integer;
                 { index of the term to be defined }
                next: pTop
                 { link to the next element of the list }
          end;
var term: array[1..max] of String;
    { term[i] = the i-th term }
    nr_pred: array[1..max] of ShortInt;
    {nr_pred[i] = number of predecessors of the i-th term}
    list_succ: array[1..max] of pTop;
    {lista_succ[i] = list of successors of the i-th term}
    n: Byte; { nr of terms }
    m: Byte; { nr of relations }
    a,b: String; { two terms in order a<b }
    i,j,k: Byte; done: Boolean; p: pTop; {dummy variables}
    k1,k2: Byte;
    {k1 = position of a in term, k2 = position of b }
```

```
begin
     WriteLn('Topological sort');
     WriteLn('******************');
     Write('Give the nr of terms: '); ReadLn(n);
     for i:=1 to n do
         begin
           Write('Give the term nr. ',i,': ');
           ReadLn(term[i]);
           nr_pred[i]:=0;
           list_succ[i]:=Nil
         end;
     Write('Give nr of relations: '); ReadLn(m);
     for i:=1 to m do
         begin
           WriteLn('Relation nr. ',i,': a<b:');
           Write('a='); ReadLn(a);
           { a si b must belong }
           Write('b='); ReadLn(b);
           { to vector term }
     { determine the position for a and for b }
           for j:=1 to n do
               begin
                 if term[j]=a then k1:=j;
                 if term[j]=b then k2:=j
               end;
     { add b to the list of the successors of a }
           New(p); p^.info:=k2;
           p^.next:=list_succ[k1];
           list_succ[k1]:=p;
           { increase nr of predecessors of b }
```

```
        nr_pred[k2]:=nr_pred[k2]+1
      end;
   { at each step display and remove from digraph first
encountered element with no predecessors: term[j] }
     for i:=1 to n do
       begin
         j:=1; done:=False;
         while (j<=n) and (not done) do
               if nr_pred[j]=0 then
                  begin
                    { display j term }
                    Write(term[j],', ');
                    done:=True;
                    { remove }
                    nr_pred[j]:=-1;
              {  for  every  element  in  the  list  of
successors for j, number of predecessors decreases by 1 }
                    p:=list_succ[j];
                    while p<>Nil do
                          begin
                           nr_pred[p^.info]:=
                             nr_pred[p^.info]-1;
                            p:=p^.next
                          end
                  end
               else
                 j:=j+1
         end;
end.
```

Chapter 3. Trees

Let $H=(V, E)$ be a digraph (a directed graph). A vertex $v_0 \in V$ will be called the root of G, so as whatever a vertex $v \in V$, there exists at least one path from v_0 to v. If $H=(V,E)$ is a digraph, then by means of the support graph of H we will understand the graph obtained from H, after dropping the orientation of the arcs. H will be called **arborescence** if it has a root and its support graph is a tree.

In informatics, the arborescences are called, by “abusing” the language, **trees**. Specifying the root and considering that the orientation of the edges (corresponding to covering the unique path from the root to each vertex) is implicit. Each vertex will have, in this way, some sons, those being the immediate neighbors on the path from the root downwards (towards the leaves, i.e. nodes without sons). A tree with maximum two sons is also called a **binary tree**.

Example:

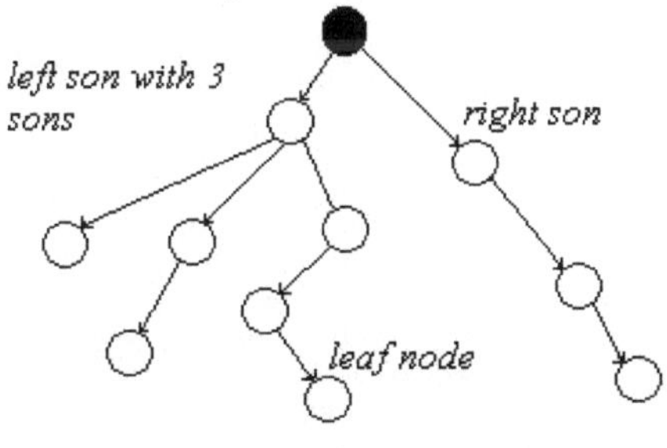

The root has two sons and the one on the left has, in its turn, three sons; leaf node; the right-hand son of the root

Looking at it in reverse order, a tree indeed resembles a real tree, in which case the names of tree, leaf and root, also, are justifiable. We notice that we can consider the tree to be organized on more levels. The first level is the root level. Then the level of the root’s sons etc., until the last one, the level of the last leaves.

Next, we will pay attention to the binary trees in particular because, like we will show later on, the study of regular trees is reduced to the study of binary trees.

3.1. Binary Trees

The reference of a binary tree and implicitly its defining will be done by means of a pointer towards its root node. Each node of the tree is a record with the following elements:

- an information `info`, integer type
- two pointers towards the two sons (the left subtree and the right subtree) of the nodes: `left` and `right`

In the following program, we will build up such trees, which have, in addition, this characteristic: each node of the tree is greater then or equal to the nodes from the left son and smaller than the nodes of the right son (from the point of view of the `info` field). A tree which respects these rules is named **search-sorting tree**.

The *search* for an element in such trees is indeed easy to do: if the searched-for element is identical to the information in the node, then the search will be successful; if not, then one of the two paths will be followed: if the searched-for element is smaller, then we will work with the left son; otherwise, the right son will be used. If one tries to go beyond a terminal node, thus to `Nil`, then the search will fail. The procedure `Search` from the next demo program returns the subtree having as root the element found in the tree that was searched for.

A binary tree can be *traversed* in three ways:

- in *inorder:* the left son is the first that is visited, recursively, in inorder, then the root, then the right son;
- in *postorder:* the left son is visited, then the right one, and in the end, the root;

- in *preorder:* the root will be visited, then the left son, and then the right one.

☞Note

The traverse in inorder of such a tree will lead to the elements from the nodes of the tree being displayed in ascending order, which is a reason why such trees should also be considered sorting trees.

If the elements `2, 5, 7, 3, 4, 9, 1, 5, 8, 0 = stop` are inserted one at a time, then the tree from the diagram below will be obtained.

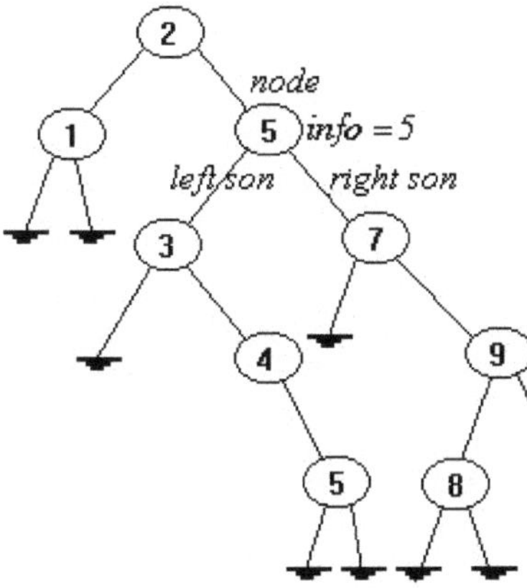

The next program implements the tree structure that was discussed about and the main operations that are done with such data structures.

```
program BinaryTrees;
type tree = ^nod;
     node = record info: Integer; left, right: tree end;
procedure Init(var A: tree);
begin A := Nil end;
{$S-}
procedure Insertion(var A: tree; elem: Integer);
var OneNode: node;
```

```
begin
  if A <> Nil then
   if elem <= A^.info then
     Insertion(A^.left, elem)
   else
     Insertion(A^.right, elem)
  else
   begin
     New(A);
     OneNode.info:=elem;
     OneNode.left:=Nil; OneNode.right:=Nil;
     A^:=OneNode
   end
end;
```

```
procedure Search(A: tree; elem: Integer; var a_node: tree);
begin
 if A = Nil then a_node := Nil
 else
   if A^.info = elem then a_node := A
   else
     if elem <= A^.info then
          Search(A^.stg, elem, a_node)
     else Search(A^.dr, elem, a_node)
end;
```

```
procedure PreOrder(A: tree);
begin
  if A <> Nil then
     begin Write(A^.info,',');
```

```
    PreOrder(A^.left); PreOrder(A^.right)
    end
end;
procedure PostOrder(A: tree);
begin
  if A <> Nil then
     begin
     PostOrder(A^.left);
    PostOrder(A^.right); Write(A^.info,',')
     end
end;
procedure InOrder(A: tree);
begin
  if A <> Nil then
     begin Inorder(A^.left);
    Write(A^.Info,','); InOrder(A^.right)
    end
end;
{$S+}
var A, B: tree; elem: Integer;
begin
  Init(A);
  repeat
    Write('Provide the element to be inserted
          (0 = stop): '); ReadLn(elem);
    if elem <> 0 then Insertion(A,elem)
  until elem = 0;
  WriteLn('The tree in preorder: ');
  PreOrder(A); WriteLn;
  WriteLn('The tree in postorder: ');
```

```
  PostOrder(A); WriteLn;
  WriteLn('The tree in inorder ',
          ' => the sorted elements: ');
  InOrder(A); WriteLn;
  repeat
    Write('Provide the searched-for element');
    Write(' (0 = stop): ');
    ReadLn(elem);
    if elem <> 0 then
      begin
        Search(A, elem, B);
        if B <> Nil then
          begin
            WriteLn('I found it,',
                    ' the tree in inorder is: ');
            InOrder(B); WriteLn
          end
        else WriteLn('I did not find it.')
      end
  until elem = 0;
end.
```

The most complicated operation in a binary search tree is deleting a node (so as the tree should keep its binary-tree characteristics).

The node to be deleted can be found one of the four hypostases (cases):

1. it has no son – in which case the father node will point towards `Nil`;
2. it only has the left son – the father node is linked with the left son of the node that will be deleted:
3. it only has the right son – the father node is linked with the right son of the node that will be deleted;
4. it has both sons – it is brought in the node that has to be deleted the

information of the node with the largest key from its left subtree, and, to the right of the father of the moved node, its left son is linked.

Example:

For the tree in the picture below, node `20` will be deleted according to rule 1- that is the easiest case. If node `15` had to be deleted, then node `19` would be directly linked to node `17`, which would become the left son of node `19`.

If, however, node `10` has to be deleted, then in the place of node `10` will be brought the node with the 'largest' information from its left subtree, therefore the information "`8`" will be the one to be brought, then node 6 will be linked to the right with node `7`.

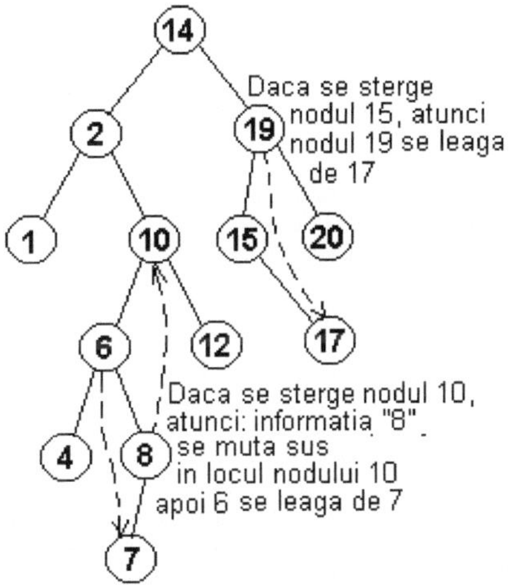

If node `15` is deleted, then node `19` is connected with `17`. If node `10` is deleted, the information "`8`" move upwards instead of node `10`, then `6` connects to `7`.

The procedure for deleting an element `elem` from tree `A` is recursive. It contains a procedure `St` to solve case `4`:

```
procedure Delete(var A: tree; elem: Integer);
var q: tree;
    procedure LeftDel(var A:tree);
```

```
    begin
         if A^.right=Nil then
            begin
              q^.info:=A^.info;
              q:=A;
              A:=A^.left;
            end
         else
            LeftDel(A^.right)
    end;
begin
     if A=Nil then
        WriteLn('The element ',elem,
                ' does not exist...')
     else
       if elem=A^.info then
          begin
            q:=A;
            if q^.left=Nil then
               A:=q^.right
            else
               if q^.right=Nil then
                  A:=q^.left
               else
                 St(q^.left);
            Dispose(q)
          end
      else
          if elem<A^.info then
             Delete(A^.left,elem)
```

```
        else
           Delete(A^.right,elem)
end;
```

As an exercise, you can modify the presented program so that it should also contain the `Delete` procedure, which should be used for deleting different tree nodes.

3.2. The Binary Tree Associated with an Algebraic Expression

Any arithmetic or algebraic expression can be memorized by means of a binary tree. Each node of the tree will be either an operator or an operand. The operators will have two sons which are their operands. The functions represent a special case; they will have only one son (the left son for example). The operands will have no son.

Consequently, for a random arithmetic expression, we can obtain its associated binary tree. For example, for the expression `x*sin(x^2)` the binary tree will be:

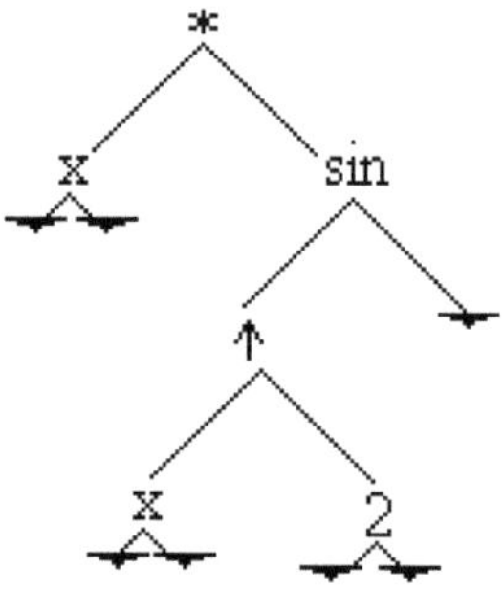

- the unary functions, like `sin` in this case will have the right son `nil` and the numbers and `x` will have both sons `nil`;
- the post-fixed form associated with this tree is : `x x 2 ^ sin *`.

In this way an expression will be represented by means of the binary tree which corresponds to the post-fixed form of the expression.

We will use a binary arborescent structure. In order to transform a regular expression into a tree, we will use two stacks, one of the operators and functions (which can be considered as being unary operators), and the other- of the operands, which will be smaller trees. Larger trees will be formed from these smaller trees using as root the element that could be found at the top of the operators' stack at that time.

Let's see how we are going to deal with the expression `2+x^3`.

We will introduce into the operators' stack the small tree $/^{2}\backslash$ (and not the number 2), then into the operators' stack + and the tree $/^{x}\backslash$ into the operands' stack.

Notice that ^ (raise to power) has a higher priority than +, thus we will not do 2 + x, instead we will also introduce ^ into the operators' stack, then $/^{3}\backslash$ into the operands' stack.

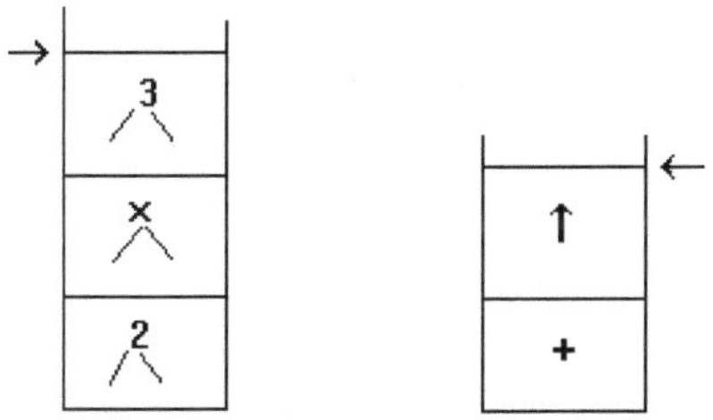

OPERANDS OPERATORS

Now we have to take the two small trees out of the stack and to form a new tree having the operator ^ (that was taken out of the operators' stack) as root:

which will be introduced into the operands' stack:

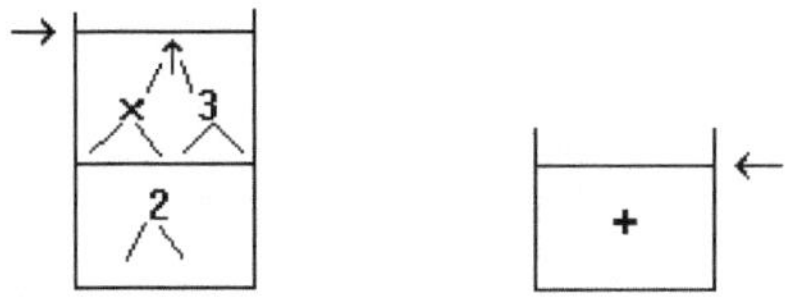

OPERANDS OPERATORS

The only remaining operation is + and, by following the same steps like before, we obtain:

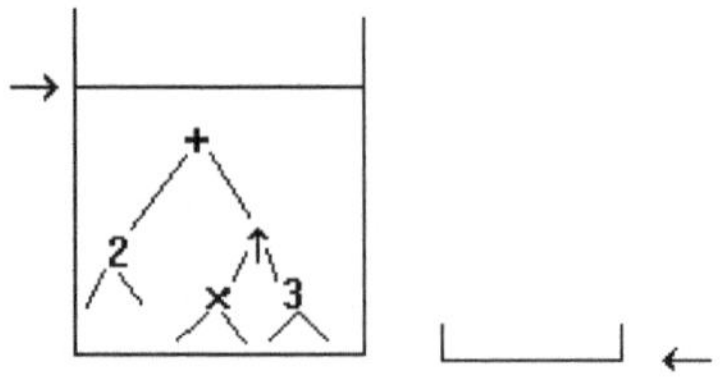

OPERANDS OPERATORS

At that moment the operators' stack is empty, and the operands' stack contains the binary tree associated with the given expression.

Attention

Special problems arise when on top of the stack of the operations is – or /, and the successive operation (in the expression) is also -, respectively, /. (These symbols represent noncommutative operations.)

The following program does these transformations.

The display of the resulting binary tree is done graphically. (The DOS path to the file EGAVGA.BGI, from the *Turbo-Pascal* package, has to be known. We consider that this is "`C:\BP\BGI`".)

```
program TheTreeAssociatedWithAnAlgebraicExpression;
uses Graph,Crt;
const lmax = 3; vmax = 50;
type expression =  string; information  =  string[lmax];
     vector =  record
          info:array[1..vmax] of information; nr:1..vmax
         end;
     tree  =  ^node;
     node  =  record
                info:information; left,right:tree
              end;
var the_expression, expr_fpo: expression;
    the_vector: vector;
    the_tree: tree;
```

```
procedure OpenGraph;
var gd,gm: Integer;
begin
  gd:= Detect; InitGraph(gd,gm,'C:\BP\BGI');
              {the path of the file EGAVGA.BGI}
end;
procedure Vectorize(expr: expression; var vec: vector);
    procedure Change(var x, y: information);
    var a: information;
    begin a := x; x := y; y := a end;
var i,j,k: Integer;
begin
  i := 0; k := 0;
  while i<Length(expr) do
    begin
      Inc(i);
      if expr[i] in ['s','c','l','e'] then
         begin
           Inc(k);
           if expr[i]<>'l' then
              vec.info[k]:=expr[i]+expr[i+1]+expr[i+2]
           else
              vec.info[k] := expr[i]+expr[i+1]+' ';
           if expr[i] = 'l' then Inc(i)
           else
             begin
               vec.info[k] := vec.info[k]+expr[i+2];
               Inc(i,2)
             end
         end
```

```
      else
        if expr[i] in ['(',')','+','-','*','/','^','x']
           then
           begin Inc(k); vec.info[k] := expr[i] end
        else
         begin { figures };
           Inc(k); vec.info[k] := '         '; j := 1;
           while not (expr[i] in ['(',')','+','-','*',
                '/','^','s','c','l','e']) do
           begin
             vec.info[k][j] := expr[i];
             Inc(i); Inc(j)
           end;
           Dec(i)
        end
    end;
  vec.nr := k
end;
```

procedure MTree(vec: vector; var arb: tree);

```
const topmax = 25;
var i,top1,top2: Integer;
    operator: array[1..topmax] of String[lmax];
    operand: array[1..topmax] of tree;
  function priority(op:char):byte;
  begin
    case op of
         '(',')':priority := 0; '+','-':priority := 1;
         '*','/':priority := 2; '^':priority := 3;
         's','c','l','e':priority := 4
    end
```

```
  end;
begin { tree-ize }
  i := 0; top1 := 0; top2 := 1; operator[top2] := '(';
  while (i<=vec.nr) and (top2>0) do
    begin { 1 }
      Inc(i);
      if vec.info[i][1] in ['x','0'..'9'] then
         begin
           Inc(top1); New(arb);
           arb^.info := vec.info[i];
           arb^.stg := nil; arb^.dr := nil;
           operand[top1] := arb;
         end
      else
        if vec.info[i][1]='(' then
        begin Inc(top2);operator[top2]:='(' end
        else
         begin { 2 }
           while (top2>0) and
                 (not (operator[top2][1] in ['(',')']))
                  and
                 (priority(operator[top2][1])>=
                  priority(vec.info[i][1]))
             do begin
                  if operator[top2][1] in
                     ['l','c','s','e'] then
                  begin
                   New(arb);
                 arb^.info := operator[top2];
                   arb^.left := operand[top1];
```

```
                  arb^.right := nil;
                  operand[top1] := arb
                 end
                 else begin { + - * / ^ }
                        New(arb);
                        arb^.info := operator[top2];
                        arb^.left:=operand[top1-1];
                        arb^.right:=operand[top1];
                        operand[top1-1]:=arb; Dec(top1)
                      end;
                Dec(top2)
              end; { while - 2}
         if top2>0 then
            if (operator[top2] <> '(') or
               (vec.info[i][1] <> ')') then
               begin
                 Inc(top2);
                 operator[top2]:=vec.info[i]
               end
            else Dec(top2)
     end; { else ...}
end; { while }
if (i=vec.nr) and (top2=0) then
   begin
     New(arb);
     arb := operand[1]
   end
else
   begin
     New(arb);
```

```
      arb^.info:='old';
      arb^.left:=nil;
      arb^.right:=nil
    end
end;
{$S-}
procedure Type1(arb: tree; level,x0: Integer);
const dy=30;
var i, dx: Integer;
begin
  dx := GetMaxX; for i := 1 to nivel do dx := dx div 2;
  if arb=nil then OutTextXY(x0+dx, level*dy, #207)
  else begin
         OutTextXY(x0+dx, level*dy, arb^.info);
         Line(x0+dx, level*dy+5, x0+dx div 2,
              (level+1)*dy-5);
         Line(x0+dx, level*dy+5, x0+dx+dx div 2,
              (level+1)*dy-5);
         Type1(arb^.left,level+1,x0);
         Type1(arb^.right,level+1,x0+dx)
      end
end;
{$S+}
{$S-}
procedure Post_fixedForm(arb: tree; var expr: expression);
var expr1, expr2: expression;
begin
  expr := '';
  if arb<>nil then
     begin
```

```
      Post_fixedForm(arb^.left, expr1);
      Post_fixedForm(arb^.right, expr2);
      expr := expr1 + ' ' + expr2 + ' '+arb^.info
    end
end;
{$S+}
begin { main program }
  ClrScr; WriteLn(' Give the expression ! ');
  ReadLn(expression); expression := expression+')';
  vectorize(the_expression,the_vector); New(the_tree);
  MTree(the_vector,the_tree);
  OpenGraph; SetTextJustify(CenterText, CenterText);
  OutTextXY(GetMaxX div 2, 10,
            Copy(expression,1,Length(expression)-1));
  Post_fixedForm(the_tree, expr_fpo);
  OutTextXY(GetMaxX div 2, GetMaxY-30, expr_fpo);
  Type1(the_tree,1,0);
  Dispose(the_tree);
  ReadLn;
  CloseGraph
end.
```

Attention!

As it could be noticed from the main program, the steps of the algorithm are:

- the expression is read in normal form: the_expression;
- the expression is memorized in an array (vector), for further using;
- the tree associated with the expression is built out of this vector;

The post-fixed form of the tree is also obtained. Finally, the tree will be displayed.

3.2. Regular Trees

At the beginning of the paragraph, the notion of tree (a regular one) was defined; then we worked with binary trees (section 6.3.1).

A regular tree has more sons. This is why each node will be memorized by means of its information and a set of connections to the son-nodes. We need to know how many sons each node has and to maintain the connections towards these sons in a vector of pointers to other nodes.

```
type tree = ^node;
     node = record
               NoSons:Byte;
               info:Integer;
               son: array[1..10] of tree
             end;
```

Creating and searching within a regular tree

A regular tree can be created recursively, along with reading the information of its nodes, by means of the keyboard, like in the procedure:

```
procedure ReadT(var A: tree; no, parent: Integer);
var i: Byte;
begin
  New(A);
  Write('Give the info. for the son ',no,' of ',
         parent,': ');
  ReadLn(A^.info);
  if A^.info<>0 then
     begin
       Write('Give the number of sons',
             'for node ',A^.info, ' : ');
       ReadLn(A^.NoSons);
```

```
            for i:=1 to A^.NoSons do
                 Read(A^.son[i],i,A^.info);
          end
     else A:=nil
end;
```

Firstly, the procedure `ReadT` will be called for the root node of the entire tree: `ReadT(A,0,0)`. This will lead to the creation of a new `Nil` connection.

The arguments of the procedure are:

- `A`: pointer towards the current node from the subtree that is going to be created;
- `parent`: the information from the parent node of the current node;
- `nr`: the number of the current node as a son of the parent node;

For example, for the case displayed in the figure below, if this procedure is employed for the subtree whose root is in node 4, then we will have:

- `A`= pointer towards node `4`;
- `parent`= node `1`;
- `nr = 3`, because node `4` is the third son of parent node `1`.

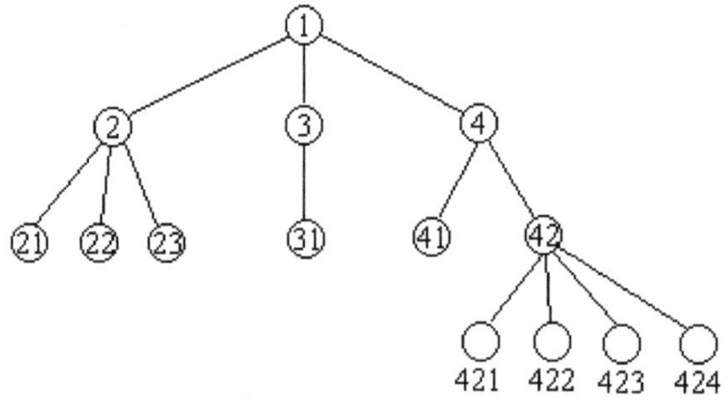

We propose that the reader should create a procedure which performs a depth traversal and search for an element in such a tree.

Storing Regular Trees by Means of Binary Trees

A regular tree can be stored by means of a binary tree.

Let's consider a regular tree with integers as nodes information:

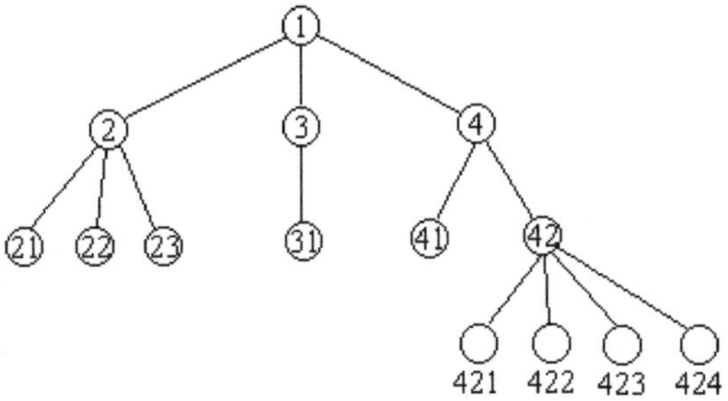

We notice that we can link the root `1` with node `2`, and then node `2` can be linked with its first son (`21`). The following son of the root, with label `3`, it could be named as a *brother* of `2`.

By doing this for all the nodes in the tree, we will obtain a binary tree, with two connections:

- the one on the left being with the first son.
- the one on the right with the first brother of the right-hand side of this son.

In this way, the tree from the previous figure will be memorized in the binary tree below:

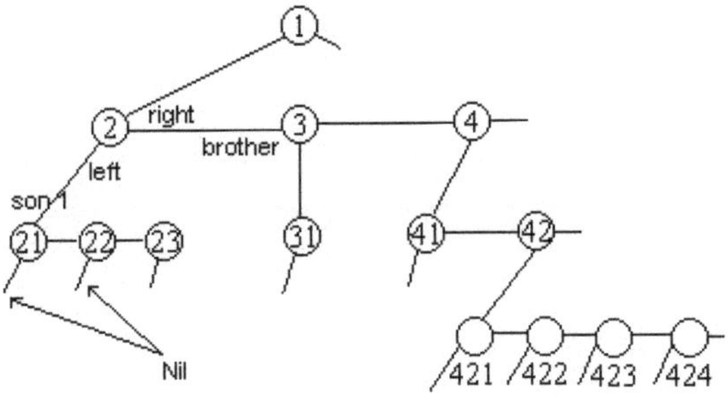

A demo program will be presented which will do the following:

- it will read a regular tree `A` from the keyboard;
- it will display this tree vertically, just in the way in which the directories

(folders) structure is displayed as result of a "TREE" command;

- it will store the tree `A` in the form of a binary tree `A2` (the `tree2` type);
- it will display the `A2` tree in a similar manner.

Concerning the procedures that execute these operations of the program, the following must be mentioned:

- the manner in which the `ReadT` procedure takes over from the keyboard the data about a regular tree `A` is the following: the information from a node (the root node) is read first; then, the number of sons this node has; for each son this procedure will be recursively used, by reading the subtrees that have as roots those particular sons;
- the `TypingInPreorder` procedure (and its particular case determined by `TypingInPreorder2` procedure as well) uses special graphical characters for drawing the tree structure. These special graphical characters form different *headers,* which are displayed before a node. (These headers can be spaces or headers of vertical symbols, which means that we find ourselves on an inferior level, or even headers depending on the number of the node, as a son of its father. The asterisk ('`*`') symbolizes `Nil`.);
- the `TransfTree` procedure is the most important. It is the one which transforms a regular tree `A` into a binary tree `A2`. The procedure is recursive and it is called for the first son of root `A` (labeled as `son1`), and for all the other sons as well (between `2` and `NoSons`), which will be linked with one another on the right-hand side in the `A2` tree.

```
program TransformRegularTreeIntoBinaryTree;
uses Crt;
const max=10;
type tree = ^node;
     node=record
           NoSons:Byte;
           info:Integer;
```

```
          son: array[1..10] of tree
        end;
    tree2 = ^node2;
    node2 = record
              info: Integer; left,right: tree2
            end;
```

```
procedure TransfTree(a: tree; var a2: tree2);
var son1:tree; c,b,d: tree2; i: Byte;
begin
  if a<>Nil then
    begin
      New(a2);
      a2^.info:=a^.info;
      a2^.left:=Nnil;
      a2^.right:=Nil;
      if a^.NoSons>0 then
        begin
          son1:=a^.son[1]; TransfTree(son1,b);
          a2^.left:=b; d:=b;
          for i:=2 to a^.NoSons do
              begin
                TransfTree(a^.son[i],c);
                b^.right:=c; b:=b^.right
              end
        end
    end
  else
    a2:=nil
end;
```

```
procedure TypingInPreorder2(A: tree2);
const left=#195#196#196;
      right=#192#196#196;
      vertical=#179#32#32;
      MaxLevels=20;
var header: array[1..MaxLevels] of String;
    k: Integer;
  procedure Tpreorder(current: tree2);
  var i: Integer;
  begin
    for i:=0 to k do
        Write(header[i]);
    if current<>nil then
       WriteLn(current^.info)
    else WriteLn('*');
    if current<>Nil then
       if (current^.left<>Nil) or (current^.right<>Nil)
          then
          if k<MaxLevels then
             begin
               if header[k]=left then
                  header[k]:=vertical
               else
                  header[k]:= ' ';
               k:=k+1; header[k]:=left;
               TPreorder(current^.left);
               header[k]:=right;
               TPreorder(current^.right); k:=k-1
             end
  end;
```

```
begin
  k:=0;
  header[k]:= '-->';
  TPreorder(A)
end;
procedure ReadT(var A: tree; no, parent: Integer);
var i: Byte;
begin
  New(A);
  Write('Info for son ',no, ' of ',
        parent, ': ');
  ReadLn(A^.info);
  if A^.info<>0 then
     begin
       Write('Nr of sons for node ',A^.info, ' : ');
       ReadLn(A^.NoSons);
       for i:=1 to A^.NoSons do
           ReadT(A^.son[i],i,A^.info);
     end
  else
     A:=Nil
end;
procedure TypingInPreorder(A: tree);
const left=#195#196#196;
      right=#192#196#196;
      vertical=#179#32#32;
      MaxLevels=20;
var header: array[0..MaxLevels] of String[3];
    k: Integer;
  procedure Tpreorder(current: tree);
```

```
  var j,i: Integer;
  begin
    for i:=0 to k do
        Write(header[i]);
    if current<>nil then
       WriteLn(current^.info)
    else
       WriteLn('*');
    if current<>nil then
       if current^.NoSons>0 then
          if k<MaxLevels then
             begin
               if header[k]=left then
                  header[k]:=vertical
               else
                  header[k]:='   ';
               k:=k+1;
               for j:=1 to current^.NoSons-1 do
                   begin
                     header[k]:=left;
                     TPreorder(current^.son[j])
                   end;
               header[k]:=right;
               with current^ do
                    TPreorder(son[NoSons]);
               k:=k-1
             end
  end;
begin
  k:=0;
```

```
  header[k]:='-->';
  TPreorder(A)
end;
var A: tree; A2: tree2;
begin
  ClrScr; ReadT(A,0,0);
  TypingInPreorder(A);
  TransfTree(A,A2);  TypingInPreorder2(A2);
  ReadLn
end.
```

Here is an example of how the previous program works in relation to the regular tree considered in the previous figure:

```
Info for son 0 of 0: 1
Nr of sons for node 1: 3
Info for son 1 of 1: 2
Nr of sons for node 2 : 3
Info for son 1 of 2: 21
Nr of sons for node 21 : 0
Info for son 2 of 2: 22
Nr of sons for node 22 : 0
Info for son 3 of 2: 23
Nr of sons for node 23 : 0
Info for son 2 of 1: 3
Nr of sons for node 3 : 1
Info for son 1 of 3: 31
Nr of sons for node 31 : 0
Info for son 3 of 1: 4
Nr of sons for node 4 : 2
Info for son 1 of 4: 41
Nr of sons for node 41 : 0
```

```
Info for son2 of 4: 42
Nr of sons for node l 42 : 4
Info for son 1 of 42: 421
Nr of sons for node 421 : 0
Info for son 2 of 42: 422
Nr of sons for node 422 : 0
Info for son 3 of 42: 423
Nr of sons for node 423 : 0
Info for son 4 of 42: 424
Nr of sons for node 424 : 0
-->1
   +--2
   ¦  +--21
   ¦  +--22
   ¦  +--23
   +--3
   ¦  +--31
   +--4
      +--41
      +--42
         +--421
         +--422
         +--423
         +--424
-->1
   +--2
   ¦  +--21
   ¦  ¦  +--*
   ¦  ¦  +--22
   ¦  ¦     +--*
```

```
¦  ¦     +--23
¦  +--3
¦     +--31
¦     +--4
¦        +--41
¦        ¦  +--*
¦        ¦  +--42
¦        ¦     +--421
¦        ¦     ¦  +--*
¦        ¦     ¦  +--422
¦        ¦     ¦     +--*
¦        ¦     ¦     +--423
¦        ¦     ¦        +--*
¦        ¦     ¦        +--424
¦        ¦     +--*
¦        +--*
+--*
```

3.3. Viewing the Arborescent Structure of Directories

We will make together a program which will display the arborescent structure of directories as a practical and interesting use of regular trees. The root will be in the current directory, from the current drive. In this way, the program will work similarly with the DOS command TREE.

We will build, keeping in mind the previous program, the tree associated with the structure of those certain directories, and then we will display this tree in preorder, vertically.

The nodes of the tree will be the names of the directories. In order to see the subdirectories of a certain directory (in which we find ourselves at a certain moment), two special procedures will be used (FindFirst and FindNext). These will find the first and the next directory — which has a certain format or type — from the current directory.

Only those nodes whose feature contains the directory identifier will be selected (because from this point of view of the operating system, a directory is still a file which has a certain special feature).

Attention!

The directories '.' and '..' that correspond to the current directory, respectively to the parent directory, will be exceptions.

The current subdirectories will be the sons of the node that corresponds to the current directory. Then, with the help of ChDir procedure, we will change the directory, by moving from the current node into one of its sons. For this son node the corresponding subtree will be built, in the same way, (this son will be the root of the new tree).

Next, we will go back to the parent of the subdirectory (using ChDir ('..')); then, to the next son, for which we will do the same thing, and so on, until there is no son left.

The recursive procedure which builds the tree with the root in a directory is called Build. It will be activated from the main program for the current directory. At the end, when the entire tree is built, this is displayed with the TypingInPreorder procedure, which, in its turn, contains a recursive subprocedure- Preorder.

In the following, we will present the actual program and will comment on different uses of the procedures from the DOS package, which were called in it.

```
program MyTree;
uses Dos;
const max=500;
type TipInfo = String[12]; { the information from the
nodes of the tree is a file name, along with the
extension }
```

```
    tree = ^node;
    node = record
             info: TipInfo; NoSons: Byte;
             son: array[1..max] of tree
           end;
procedure TypingInPreorder(A: tree);
const left=#195#196#196#196;
      right=#192#196#196#196;
      vertical=#179#32#32#32;
      MaxLevels=20;
var header: array[0..MaxLevels] of String[4];
    k: Integer;
  procedure TPreorder(current: tree);
  var j,i: Integer;
  begin
    for i:=0 to k do
        Write(header[i]);
    if current<>nil then
       WriteLn(current^.info)
    else
       WriteLn('*');
     { it would have never displayed }
    if current<>nil then
       if current^.NoSons>0 then
          if k<MaxLevels then
             begin
               if header[k]=left then
                  header[k]:=vertical
               else
                  header[k]:=#32#32#32#32;
```

```
                { four spaces }
            k:=k+1;
            for j:=1 to current^.NoSons-1 do
                begin
                  header[k]:=left;
                  { for the first sons }
                  TPreorder(current^.son[j])
                end;
      header[k]:=right; { the last son }
      TPreorder(current^.son[current^.NoSons]);
      k:=k-1
   end {TPreorder }
  end;
begin
  k:=0;
  header[k]:='--> ';
  TPreorder(A)
end;
```

The `Build` procedure will search using `FindFirst` and `FindNext`, all the `FisDirector` files from the current directory (thus, with the mask '`*.*`'), which have directories (have the *Directory* feature).

The current directory will be found by calling `GetDir (0, P)` where `P` is a variable of `PathStr` type, that means a string of characters corresponding to the current path, and `0` is a constant associated with a certain disk drive: `0` = the current unity, `1`=*A*, `2`=*B* etc..

Excepting the string `P` (representing the current path), only the name of the directory and its extension (if the directory has an extension) are of interest to us. In this way, `P` will be split in more substrings by means of `FSplit(P,D,N,E)`, obtaining `D` = the path to the parent directory inclusively, and `N` and `E` will represent the names of the directory and, respectively, its extension. The latter ones will combine to obtain the information that is going to be attached to the root node of the tree: `A^.info:=N+E`.

Once the current directory is found, all of its sons will be searched for with the sequence:

- determine the first son, if exists:

```
FindFirst('*.*', Directory, FisDirector);
```

- as long as there is another son (fact signaled by the 0 value in the system variable `DosError`, which is declared in the DOS library):

```
While DosError = 0 do
      begin
```

- assign the name of the physical file `FisDirector` to the file variable `F` and determine its features (with the `GetFAttr` procedure):

```
Assign(F, FisDirector.Name); GetFAttr(F,Attr);
```

- if the directory feature is among these features (the `Directory` constant value `16`, declared in the DOS unit), and the directory is neither '.' nor '..', then the directory file will be added to the root of the tree:

```
if (Attr and Directory<>0) and
   (FisDirector.Name<>'.') and
   (FisDirector.Name<>'..') then
    begin
      Inc(A^.NoSons);  New(A^.son[A^.NoSons]);
      A^.son[A^.NoSons]^.info:=FisDirector.Name
    end;
```

- then move on to search for the next file which matches the desired template:

```
FindNext(FisDirector)
      end;
```

Finally, each of the son-subdirectories will be traversed and the recursive method will still be called in order to further build the arborescent structure.

The complete procedure and the main program are further presented.

```
procedure Build(var A: tree);
var FisDirector: SearchRec; F: File; Attr: Word;
  { that means integer number between 0 and 65535 }
  P: PathStr; { String[80] } D: DirStr; { String[67] }
  N: NameStr; { String[8] } E: ExtStr; { String[4] }
  i: Integer;
begin
     A^.NoSons:=0; GetDir(0,P);
     FSplit(P,D,N,E); A^.info:=N+E;
     FindFirst('*.*', Directory, FisDirector);
     while DosError = 0 do
       begin
         Assign(F,FisDirector.Name); GetFAttr(F,Attr);
         if (Attr and Directory<>0) and
            (FisDirector.Name<>'.')
            and (FisDirector.Name <> '..') then
            begin
              Inc(A^.NoSons); New(A^.son[A^.NoSons]);
              A^.son[A^.NoSons]^.info
                 :=FisDirector.Name
            end;
         FindNext(FisDirector)
       end;
     for i:=1 to A^.NoSons do
         begin
           ChDir(A^.son[i]^.info);
           Build(A^.son[i]); ChDir('..')
         end
end;
var A: tree; Path: PathStr;
```

```
begin
    New(A); GetDir(0,Path);
    WriteLn('The tree of the directory ',Path);
    Build(A); TypingInPreorder(A); WriteLn
end.
```

After this program is carried out, an arborescent structure of the following type will be displayed:

```
The tree of the directory C:\MSOFFICE
--> MSOFFICE
    ├──SETUP
    │   └──MS-BTTNS
    ├──WINWORD
    │   ├──TEMPLATE
    │   ├──MACROS
    │   ├──STARTUP
    │   ├──LETTERS
    │   └──WORDCBT
    ├──EXCEL
    │   └──LIBRARY
    │       └──MSQUERY
    └──CLIPART
        └──PCSFILES
```

As an exercise, we suggest you make a similar program in which the regular files contained in the directories will be displayed also (with small caps and after the son-subdirectories).

Questions

1 ☺ For a given a list of integers create a list that must have only even numbers from the first list. Then, concatenate the two lists.

2 ☺ For a given stack, create a queue by extracting an element from the stack and by putting it in the queue.

3 ☺ Sort alphabetically a text file by taking the lines of the file in a dynamic list (single or double chained).

4 ☺ Write a program that can create in preorder the nodes of a tree, every node being followed by the list of his two sons included in brackets. For example, for the above tree we have this list: `a(b (d (#,#),e(#,#)), c(#, f(#,#)).`

The symbol # describes the `Nil` pointer.

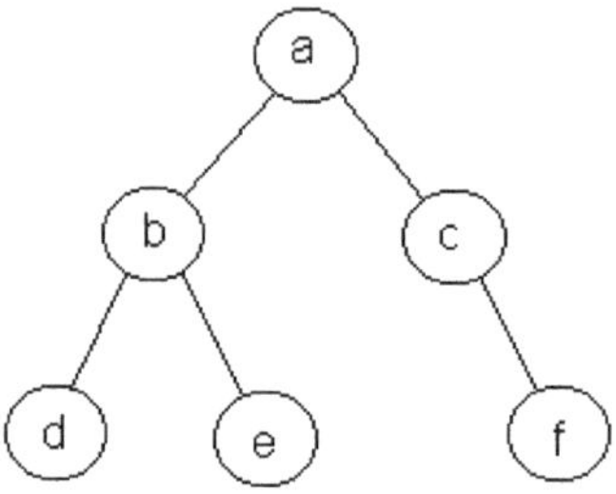

5 ☹ For the previous question, dynamically create the list instead of just displaying it.

6 ☹ A binary tree is given and the information from the nodes is the names of some people. The tree is create recursively in preorder, using the following rule: if you use `#,` then there is `Nil`; if not then you put the used information (the name of somebody) and make use of the ´´create´´ procedure for the left son and for the right son. For this type of tree, write a function that can verify if two persons are brothers or not.

For the next instance there is a tree that was created in preorder with the following words: *Ion*, *Dana*, *Mihai*, #, #, #, *George*, *Cristina*, #, #, *Viorel*, #, *Adrian*, #, #.

Cristina and Wiliam are brothers like Dana and George, while Viorel and Mihai are not. (Different names of persons are considered).

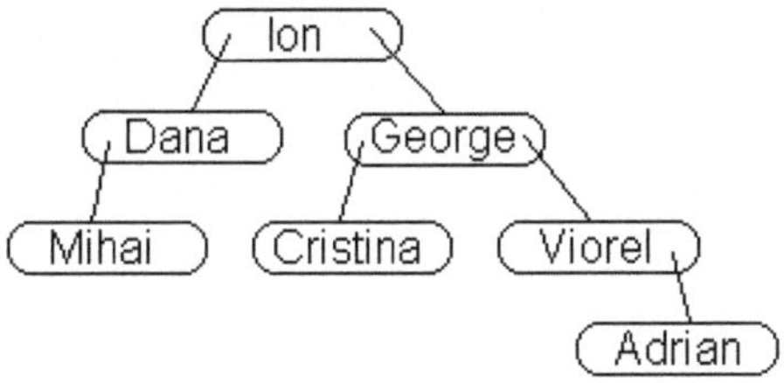

7 💣 Write a program that can evaluate a mathematical expression which contains only brackets and sum, difference, multiplication and division operators and real numbers. Two dynamically-implemented stacks will be used one for operands and the other one for operators.

8 💣A special case of random trees is the one of the multi-path trees where every node has a vector with many components and a series of pointers towards other tree nodes. They are also called B trees.

For these kind of nodes, we have the following declaration:

```
const max=10;
type BTree = ^node;
     node = record
            n: Byte;
            son: array[0..max] of BTree;
            info: array[1..max] of Integer
          end;
```

In every tree node the following conditions are considered checked:

•`son[i]<=info[i+1], ∀i=1,n-1;`

•`son[i]=Nil, ∀i=n+1,max;`

•`if son[i-1]≠Nil and/or son[i]≠Nil then:`

`son[i-1]^.info[j]≤info[i]≤son[i]^.info[k],`

`∀i=1,n, ∀j=1,son[i-1]^.n; ∀k=1,son[i]^.n.`

In other words, the elements which contain information from each node are sorted ascending. Between any two consecutive elements there is a pointer to a node, that, if it is not `Nil`, then it contains elements between the two elements within the given node. Also, there is a pointer at the beginning towards the smaller elements than the first element from the node, and also a pointer at the end through the bigger elements than the last element from the node.

Here is an example:

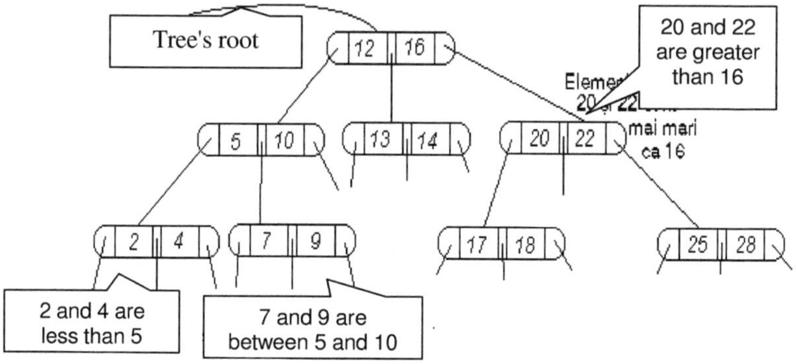

Write procedures that can create such a tree, search for an element, display it graphically or delete it.

9 Create a dynamic structure for a matrix, then rotate this matrix with 90 degrees on counterclockwise.

10 Same problem, but obtain the mirror of the matrix according to its central vertical axis.

Conclusions

1. The Turbo Pascal Language allows creating dynamic variables for which memory is allocated in the heap zone. They correspond to referential static variables, called "pointers".

2. New(p) determine ``memory allocation`` for a dynamic variable referred by referential variable ´´p´´. The release of that memory space is made with Dispose (p).

3. Auto-referencing data structures can be defined by using pointers. These are the simple or doubly-linked lists and the trees.

4. A particular case of simple lists are the stacks, which work using the LIFO mechanism. Another particular case is represented by queues that work using the FIFO mechanism.

5. The specific operations for lists are: traverse and display remove, insert or add an element.

6. Binary trees are particular examples of trees, in which every node stores information and two pointers to two descendents, the left son and the right son. The study of random trees can be reduced to the study of binary trees.

7. A particular case of binary trees is the search trees, in which the information from every node is larger than the information from the left son's node and smaller than or equal to the one from right son's node.

BIBLIOGRAPHY

1. Valentin Cristea, Irina Athanasiu, Eugenia Kalisz, Lorina Negreanu - Borland Pascal 7.0 pentru Windows, Ed. Teora, Bucureşti, 1994.

2. Doina Rancea - Limbajul Turbo Pascal, Ed. Libris, Cluj-Napoca, 1995.

3. Sorin Tudor - Turbo Pascal. Algoritmi şi limbaje de programare, Ed. Teora, Bucureşti, 1995.

4. Ovidiu Pavel, Maria Bouruc - Mediul de programare Pascal. Manualul limbajului,
Bucureşti, 1986.

5. Fl. Munteanu, T. Ionescu, Gh. Muscă, Daniela Tătaru, S. M. Dascălu – Programarea calculatoarelor. Manual pentru licee de informatică, cl. X-XII, Ed. Didactică şi Pedagogică, Bucureşti, 1994.

6. Kovacs Sandor, Turbo Pascal 6.0 - Ghid de utilizare, Ed. MicroInformatica, Cluj-Napoca, 1991.

7. Makkai Andras, Cecilia Crişan, Kovacs Sandor - Ghid de utilizare Turbo Pascal
5.0-5.5, Ed. Romanian Software Comp. (MicroInformatica), Cluj-Napoca, 1991.

8. Winfried Kassera, Volker Kassera - Programarea în Turbo Pascal 6.0, Ed. Tipomur,
Târgu Mureş, 1992.

9. Lucian Vasiu, Radu Grama, Alexandra Aldica - Programare avansată în Turbo
Pascal 6.0, Ed. MicroInformatica, Cluj-Napoca, 1993.

10. Grigore Albeanu - Programarea în Pascal, Turbo Pascal. Culegere de probleme,
Ed. Tehnică, Bucureşti, 1994.

11. Dorel Lucanu - Proiectarea algoritmilor. Tehnici elementare, Ed. Universității "Al.
I. Cuza", Iaşi, 1993.

12. Adrian Atanasiu - Concursuri de informatică. Probleme propuse, Ed. Petrion,
Bucureşti, 1995.

13. Victor Mitrana - Provocarea algoritmilor. Probleme pentru concursurile de informatică, Ed. Agni, Bucureşti, 1994.

14. Leon Livovschi, Horia Georgescu - Sinteza şi analiza algoritmilor, Ed. Ştiinţifică şi
Enciclopedică, Bucureşti, 1986.

15. Valentin Cristea, Irina Atanasiu. Eugenia Kalisz, Valeriu Iorga - Tehnici de programare, Ed. Teora, Bucureşti, 1993.

16. Sorin Tudor - Tehnici de programare, Ed. Teora, Bucureşti, 1994.

17. Cornelius Croitoru - Tehnici de bază în optimizarea combinatorie, Ed. Universităţii
“Al. I. Cuza”, Iaşi, 1992.

18. Ioan Tomescu - Bazele informaticii. Manual pentru clasa a X-a, Ed. Didactică şi
Pedagogică, Bucureşti, 1994.

19. Clara Ionescu, Ioan Zsako - Structuri arborescente cu aplicaţiile lor, Ed. Tehnică,
Bucureşti, 1990.

20. Bogdan Pătruţ - Grafică în OOP ...şi nu numai..., Ed. Adias, Râmnicu Vâlcea, 1995.

21. Bogdan Pătruţ - Învăţaţi limbajul Pascal în 12 lecţii, Editura Teora, Bucureşti, 1997

22. * * * - Fido Pascal Conference, BBS, 1994.

23. * * * - FE - A stroke font editor, Borland International, 1994.

24. * * * - Autodesk FLI file format, Autodesk, 1995.

25. * * * - Info-Star 1/1995, Ed. Libris, Cluj-Napoca, 1995.

MIX
Papier aus verantwortungsvollen Quellen
Paper from responsible sources
FSC® C105338

Printed by Books on Demand GmbH, Norderstedt / Germany